Canadian ♦ Decades
1950s

Written By
Rennay Craats

Published by Weigl Educational Publishers Limited
6325 10th Street SE
Calgary, Alberta
T2H 2Z9

Website: www.weigl.ca
Copyright ©2012 WEIGL EDUCATIONAL PUBLISHERS LIMITED
All rights reserved. No part of this publication may be reproduced, stored in a retrieval system, or transmitted in any form or by any means, electronic, mechanical, photocopying, recording, or otherwise, without the prior written permission of the publisher.

Library and Archives Canada Cataloguing in Publication

Hacker, Carlotta, 1931-
　　1950 / Carlotta Hacker.

(Canadian decades)
Includes index.
ISBN 978-1-77071-715-2 (bound).--ISBN 978-1-77071-726-8 (pbk.)

　　1. Canada--History--1945-1963--Juvenile literature. 2. Nineteen fifties--Juvenile literature. 3. Canada--Miscellanea--Juvenile literature.
I. Title. II. Series: Canadian decades

FC615.H34 2011　　　　　j971.063'3　　　　C2011-904758-6

Printed in the United States of America in North Mankato, Minnesota
1 2 3 4 5 6 7 8 9 0 15 14 13 12 11

082011
WEP040711

Project Coordinator: Karen Durrie
Design: Terry Paulhus

Photograph Credits
Alamy: pages 11TL, 11TR, 11BR, 33M, 35BM, 35TL, 39T, 39BR; Canadian Football Hall of Fame: pages 28B; CBC Still Photo Collection: page 13B; City of Ottawa Archives: page 23M; Canadian Press Images: pages 8, 9, 17B, 22B, 24, 29B, 39TR; Getty Images: pages 10, 11TL, 16, 17T, 18, 19, 27R, 27BL, 31T, 32, 33T, 34, 34BL, 38; Glenbow Museum Archive: page 12B; National Archives of Canada: pages 11B, 12T, 13TL, 22T, 23BL, 23BR, 25M, 36, 43BL; Multicultural History Society of Ontario: page 37BR; Tech Sgt. Donald L. Wetterman: page 43T.

Every reasonable effort has been made to trace ownership and to obtain permission to reprint copyright material. The publishers would be pleased to have any errors or omissions brought to their attention so that they may be corrected in subsequent printings.

We acknowledge the financial support of the Government of Canada through the Canada Book Fund for our publishing activities.

Canadian Decades
1950s

CONTENTS

Introduction 4
Timeline 6
Disasters 8
Entertainment 10
Trends 14
World Events 16
Political Issues 20
Literature 24
Science and Technology 26
Sports 28
Economy 32
Fashion 34
Immigration 36
Music and the Arts 38
Society 40
Canada/U.S. Relations 42
Activities 44
Glossary 46
Learning More 47
Index 48

Introduction

What happened in Canada during the 1950s? People everywhere swung their hips with the latest fad: the hula hoop. Families bought bigger cars and moved to the suburbs. Television began to dominate Canadian leisure hours. The list of people and events that affected Canada could go on and on.

This book tells you about Canada and Canadians during the 1950s. The 1950s were exciting years for Canada. World War II was over, and people were beginning to enjoy themselves again. Jobs were easy to find, and life seemed

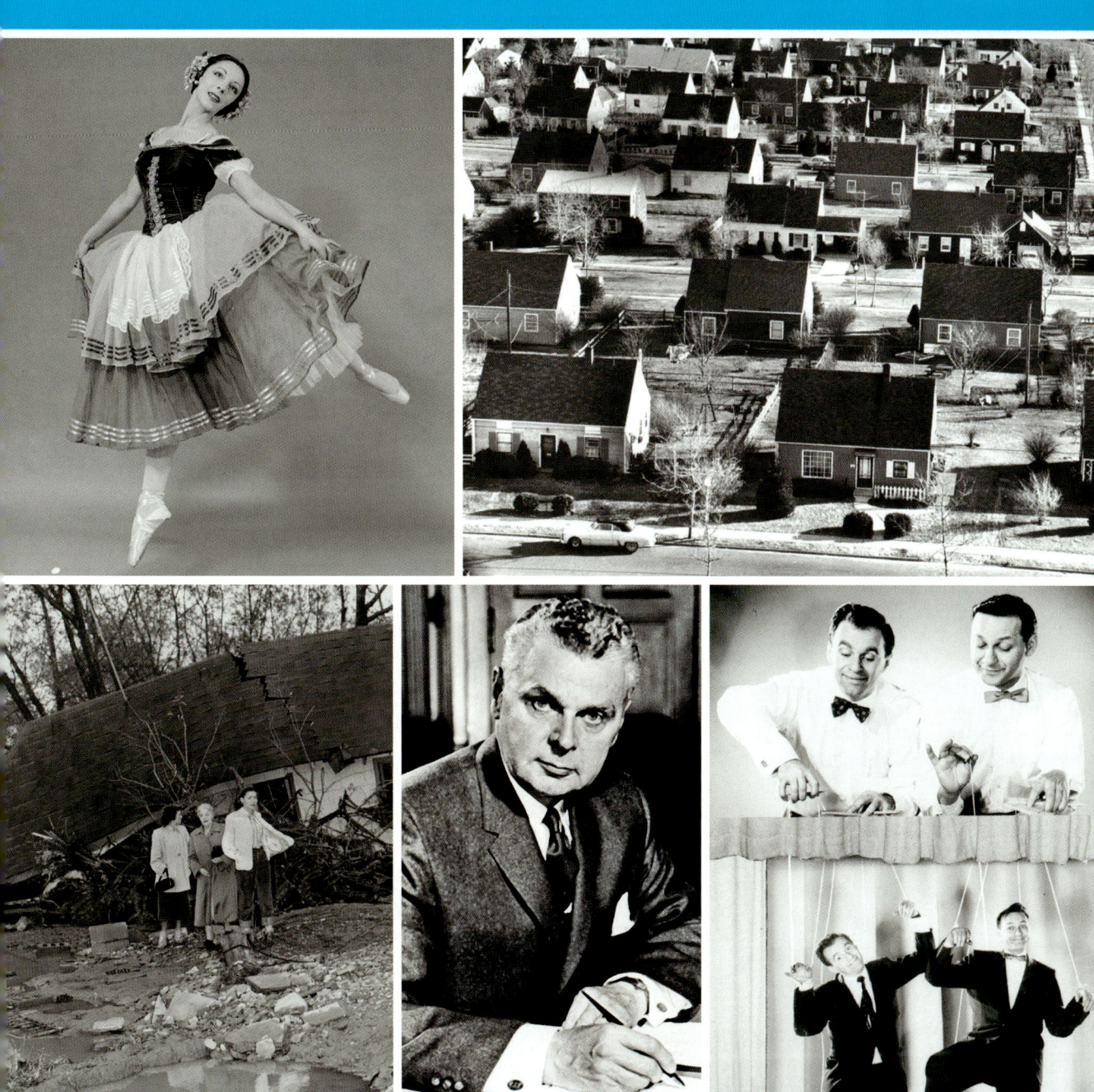

full of opportunity. Canada produced a rock star who attracted crowds as huge as those mobbing Elvis Presley. We had a world superstar political leader—Lester Pearson. Canadian inventions provided new treatments for diseases. Canada led the world in hockey and figure skating. It is not surprising that people in other countries wanted to become Canadian. Many immigrated, bringing their expertise with them.

Canadian Decades 1950s

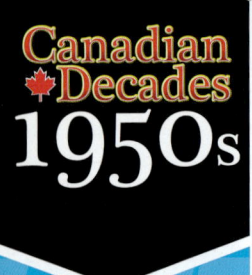

Canadian Decades
1950s

1950
The Red River keeps flowing. Despite people's efforts, the river will not be held back. (Page 9)

1951
Aboriginal people can once again perform traditional ceremonies. (Page 41)

1951
It is a year of "firsts." Thérèse Casgrain, Charlotte Whitton, and Ellen Fairclough are all famous firsts. (Page 23)

1951
Celia Franca keeps young Canadian dancers on their toes—high on their toes. (Page 13)

1951
Premier Duplessis is put in his place. Find out what a restaurateur has against the politician. (Page 20)

1952
A new Ice Age? That is what a Canadian doctor calls this life-saving technique. (Page 26)

1952
Quebec actor-playwright Gratien Gélinas is a big hit abroad as well as in Canada. (Page 11)

1953
Edmund Hillary and Tensing Norgay are on top of the world. Or at least, on top of the mountain. (Page 17)

1953
It is a big year for the Queen of England. Millions of people watch her enter the next phase in her life. (Page 16)

1953
Stratford, Ontario, welcomes a new festival to town. Find out how Alec Guinness and Richard III fit into the mix. (Page 11)

1953
Inuit are braving the elements, and it is not their idea. A large group of people are sent to live in the High Arctic. (Page 41)

1954
Canadians are asked if they can dig it. And beatniks say they certainly can. (Page 40)

1954
Scientists finally control a crippling disease. (Page 41)

1954
Slapstick comedy makes two Canadians famous. (Page 12)

6   Timeline

1955
Angry hockey fans rush into Montreal streets. Find out what Rocket Richard did to cause such a stir. (Page 29)

1955
A Canadian pianist captures Canadians' attention. He is a strange man, but he makes beautiful music. (Page 38)

1956
The list of Farley Mowat's successes is long. (Page 24)

1956
Pipeline construction turns into an uproar in 1956. (Page 21)

1957
Canada boasts a peacekeeping political leader. Lester Pearson is the first Canadian to win a prestigious award. (Page 18)

1957
He is a "whirlwind from the West!" John Diefenbaker is our new prime minister. (Page 21)

1958
An explosion rocks the deepest coal mine in North America. (Page 8)

1958
A talented Quebec poet writes a powerful novel. (Page 25)

1958
Canadians are told, in no uncertain terms, to butt out in 1958. (Page 14)

1958
Screaming fans mob Paul Anka and Elvis Presley. (Page 39)

1959
The Queen's royal yacht Britannia sails through St. Lambert Lock. (Page 27)

1959
Georges Vanier goes from war hero to Canada's governor general. (Page 23)

1959
Jacques Plante decides to take cover from flying pucks. He covers his face and starts a phenomenon. (Page 31)

1959
A blonde beauty takes over Canadian childrens' imaginations in the form of a pint-sized plastic doll. (Page 15)

Canadian Decades 1950s

Disasters

Springhill Tragedy

The coal miner was lucky to be alive. "The bump was so severe it threw me into the air," he said. He had been underground on the night of October 23, 1958, when a gas explosion blasted the Cumberland No. 2 Mine at Springhill, Nova Scotia. The "bump" was so violent that it shook the town of Springhill like an earthquake.

"I'm not hurt very much," said the miner. "But it's hard to say the chances of the others. The place is full of gas." The explosion had caused several tunnels to collapse, trapping many miners more than 3,000 metres below ground.

It was the deepest coal mine in North America. Families gathered anxiously at the mine. They had some cause for hope. Two years earlier, 88 miners had been rescued after a blast at Springhill, though 39 had died. This time, the figures were not as good. Rescue teams saved only 18 of the trapped men. Seventy-four people died in the incident.

▌Some of the Springhill miners were trapped underground for six days.

Worst Flood Since 1861

As the waters of the Red River began to rise in the spring of 1950, frantic efforts were made to prevent the river from spilling over its banks. For seven weeks, volunteers helped soldiers build **dykes** to make the banks higher. The river continued to rise, however, pouring over the surrounding Manitoba farmland. By May, almost 1,700 square kilometres were flooded, including several towns. One-sixth of Winnipeg was covered in water, and 100,000 people had to leave their homes. Experts said that if the water level had risen only 40 centimetres more, the entire population of Winnipeg would have had to flee their homes.

The disaster was a wake-up call for Manitobans. Although floods had occurred regularly in Manitoba's history, most of the province's population had never experienced one. The last severe flood had occurred in 1861.

People vowed to protect themselves against future floods. The biggest project they began was the Red River Floodway, a wide channel to take floodwater around Winnipeg. Smaller communities were protected by having dykes built in a ring around them.

■ Barricades and pumps were used to keep flood waters from spreading into downtown Winnipeg.

Hurricane Hazel

Hurricane Hazel hit south and central Ontario with a vengeance on October 15 and 16, 1954. For 24 hours, gale-force winds and rain swept across the province, battering farms, homes, bridges, and highways. Hydro wires were blown down. TV aerials were torn from roofs. A train near Southampton was rolled over. Other trains were cancelled. The violent rain caused flooding in several areas. Toronto received more than 100 millimetres of rain. By the time the storm had passed through Ontario, it had caused millions of dollars in damage and the deaths of 81 people.

■ Hurricane Hazel left thousands of people in southern Ontario homeless.

Entertainment

Quebec Winter Carnival

The people of Quebec were thrilled when the Winter Carnival became an annual event. This festival in Quebec City had begun in 1894, but had been held only occasionally. After 1955, the carnival was held each year. It quickly became the world's biggest winter celebration. There were parades and competitions, a display of snow sculptures, and various cultural and sporting events. From the beginning, a highlight was the canoe race across the partly frozen St. Lawrence River. Another major attraction was Bonhomme Carnaval, the talking snowman, who wandered among the crowds and had his own palace made of ice.

▌Quebec Winter Carnival activities include winter sports, canoe races, and snow sculptures.

Little Rooster Leads the Way

Tit-Coq, the first full-length play by Gratien Gélinas, was immensely popular. For two years, the French version played to packed audiences at Montreal's Monument National theatre. This was followed by 200 performances of the English version. In 1952, the work was made into a film, with Gélinas in the lead role. The play also achieved success on Broadway in the United States.

Tit-Coq, or "Little Rooster," was the nickname of a young army private who returns home after World War II and finds that his fiancée has married someone else. It was a story people knew all too well. The war had broken up many love affairs. *Tit-Coq*'s story clearly struck a chord with many people. French Canadians especially enjoyed the play because it was performed in Québécois French, rather than more formal Parisian French. People liked seeing and hearing about characters that were so much like themselves.

▍Gratien Gélinas' play addressed the clash between the old society and the new one that was coming out of World War II.

Spring Thaw

The New Play Society's show, *Spring Thaw*, opened with a song called We All Hate Toronto. It once included a ballet on snowshoes. The theatre production told jokes about Canada's politicians and other famous people. What could be more Canadian than *Spring Thaw*?

Spring Thaw was a **revue** that showcased Canadian talent. Early actors included Mavor Moore, Dave Broadfoot, Barbara Hamilton, and Don Harron.

The first *Spring Thaw* was thrown together in two weeks when another play was not ready. It was such a hit that it became an annual event. *Spring Thaw* ran from 1948 until 1971, and again from 1980 to 1986.

Shakespeare Comes to Ontario

Who would have thought that a theatre festival in Stratford, Ontario, would do so well so quickly? It started in a very small way in the summer of 1953. There was no theatre building—just a tent, in which rows of chairs were arranged around a stage. To attract an audience, director Tyrone Guthrie hired the famous British actor, Alec Guinness. He hired a good cast of Canadian actors, too. They opened with Shakespeare's *Richard III*. The audience loved it. From the opening night, it was clear that the project was going to be a success.

The idea of staging Shakespearean plays at Stratford had come from Tom Patterson, a local journalist. He had persuaded the town council to put some money toward the project. The summer festival did so well in its first few years that plans for a real theatre were soon under way. The beautiful new building was opened in 1957.

Canadian Cartoonist

> "After reading the papers and choosing a subject, I doodle pictorial situations."
> —Duncan Macpherson

▍Duncan Macpherson is one of Canada's most respected political cartoonists.

Canadian Decades 1950s 11

Entertainment

Wayne and Shuster

Canadians Johnny Wayne and Frank Shuster had people laughing all over North America. *The Wayne and Shuster Show* had been a Canadian Broadcasting Corporation (CBC) radio hit for many years. In 1950, the two comedians began to appear on American television.

On May 4, 1958, they performed on *The Ed Sullivan Show*, doing their most famous skit. It was about the murder of Julius Caesar, in which Caesar's wife recalls: "If I told him once, I told him a thousand times, I said, 'Julie, don't go!'" (As we know, "Julie" did go to the Forum, where he was killed.)

This was their biggest audience ever. Suddenly, Wayne and Shuster had millions of fans. "It's a mixture of **slapstick**, pantomime, visual tricks, and sheer corn," wrote one admirer.

▎Wayne and Shuster appeared on *The Ed Sullivan Show* a record 58 times.

The Manitoba Theatre Centre

The Manitoba Theatre Centre was founded in Winnipeg in 1958 by John Hirsch and Tom Hendry. It was the first regional theatre of its kind in Canada. The two directors were determined that people on the prairies should have the same cultural benefits that were available in Montreal, Toronto, Vancouver, and other big cities.

Many people in Manitoba had never seen a play performed by professional actors. Now they were able to do so. The centre also sent actors on tour and ran a theatre school for children and students. It was named by the **Canada Council** as a model for others to follow.

▎The Manitoba Theatre Centre brought many popular productions, such as *A Hatful of Rain*, to the prairies.

Celia Franca

"I would like to think of our National Ballet developing and maturing year after year until it becomes part of Canadian life." Ballerina Celia Franca made this statement in 1952, one year after founding the National Ballet of Canada.

Franca was a principal dancer until 1959, and she was artistic director until 1974. She also helped form the National Ballet School with her friend Betty Oliphant in 1959.

▎From 1959 to 1974, Franca focused on choreographing the school's programs.

Canada Council

In 1957, the Canada Council was formed, with a large fund of money to spend. The council gave out grants to promote such areas as ballet, opera, theatre, publishing, and painting. As a result, Canadians were able to enjoy a broader range of arts and entertainment.

More Canadians Watching TV

When TV broadcasting began in Canada in 1952, few families owned a television. By 1959, it was unusual not to have one.

Sports programs were particularly popular. Fans immediately found a big difference between listening to the radio report of a game and actually watching the action on TV. The same was true of drama. It was more fun to view a play than to listen to one on the radio. Most French Canadians tuned in regularly to watch *La Famille Plouffe*, a series about a Quebec working-class family.

In English-speaking Canada, *Front Page Challenge* was one of the most popular shows. Its host was Fred Davis. Pierre Berton, Gordon Sinclair, and Betty Kennedy were members of the panel that had to guess the name of the show's mystery guest.

▎*Front Page Challenge* aired for 38 years on CBC and included such guests as Eleanor Roosevelt, Indira Gandhi, and Rick Hansen.

Canadian Decades 1950s 13

Trends

Birth of the Burbs

A house, a garden, and a great big car. These were the dreams many Canadians achieved in the 1950s. With plenty of jobs available, more people than ever before could afford to buy their own home. Many chose homes in new neighbourhoods being built on the outskirts of cities—the suburbs. The suburbs were especially popular with families.

The best car to drive from the suburbs to work in the morning? It was as big and long as possible, preferably with a tail end that looked like a fish fin. Work on the Trans-Canada Highway began in the summer of 1950. What better place to drive a fin-tail car?

■ While some people complained that suburban neighbourhoods were little more than row after row of houses, Canadians flocked to the suburbs during the 1950s.

14 Trends

■ Horror movies were among the most common 3-D films during the 1950s.

3-D Movies

As cinema audiences shrank during the late 1950s, film producers searched for a way to entice TV viewers back into the theatres. They decided on a new type of film, called 3-D. Each person watching a 3-D movie was given a pair of **celluloid** glasses, which had one red lens and one green lens. When looking at a film through these glasses, everything became more real. The scenery seemed to stand out. It was not flat on the screen as in a normal movie. For a short while, 3-D movies were very popular.

Hula Hoop

Hula hoops were the latest craze. From coast to coast, young and old were swinging their hips to keep the hoops twirling.

Painters Eleven

"They are just splashing paint on canvas," some people said. "I could do better myself." Perhaps that was why not a single painting was sold when the group known as Painters Eleven held their first exhibition in 1954. Plenty of people crowded into the Roberts Gallery in Toronto to look at the paintings, but nobody bought one. Abstract art was still too new to attract many Canadians.

The group of artists had better luck in New York in 1956. In fact, they hit the jackpot. Critics raved about their pictures. The eleven painters included Jack Bush, Oscar Cahén, Hortense Gordon, Jock Macdonald, Kazuo Nakamura, William Ronald, and Harold Town.

Barbie is Here

A new doll hit the stores in 1959. Her name was Barbie. She was about 28 centimetres tall and wore the most fashionable clothes. From the moment she was put on display at the American Toy Fair in March 1959, little girls everywhere fell in love with her.

■ Harold Town began his career as an illustrator for *Maclean's* and *Mayfair* magazines.

Canadian Decades 1950s 15

World Events

Coronation of Queen Elizabeth II

In London, England, on June 2, 1953, it seemed as if the whole world had come for the **coronation** of Queen Elizabeth II. Millions of people lined the route that the new queen took in her procession to Westminster Abbey. Most of the crowd had camped on the sidewalk all night. Even the rain did not dampen their spirits. As they waited, they could hear the sound of distant cheering. Then they themselves were cheering as the marching bands and horse-drawn carriages moved past. Riding in the carriages were kings and queens, presidents and prime ministers from all over the world. Among them was the Queen of Tonga, who was given a huge cheer. She had kept the roof of her carriage pulled back, despite the pouring rain. There was more wild cheering when 27-year-old Queen Elizabeth at last came past. People felt that this was the beginning of a new era, which would be better than anything that had gone before.

▮The coronation crown of Queen Elizabeth II was originally made for the coronation of King Charles II in 1661.

Mount Everest Conquered

On May 29, 1953, Edmund Hillary of New Zealand and Tensing Norgay of Nepal became the first people ever to reach the summit of Mount Everest. As the highest mountain in the world, Everest had long challenged mountaineers. The two successful climbers were members of a British **expedition** to Mount Everest. When they reached the summit, they did what all climbers do. They shook hands, took photos, gazed at the view—and then started on the long climb back down again. Tibetans called Mount Everest *Chomolunga*, which means "mother goddess of the universe."

Korean War Ends

The Korean War began in June 1950, when **communist** soldiers from North Korea invaded South Korea. During the next three years, 25,000 Canadians served with the United Nations force that defended South Korea. Canadian soldiers gained particular respect for their brave action at a place called Kap'Yong. There, in April 1951, Princess Patricia's Canadian Light Infantry held back a powerful North Korean attack.

The war ended in July 1953, when both sides agreed to stop fighting. Then, a 4-kilometre-wide **demilitarized zone** was created between North and South Korea.

▌The Korean War was the first time the United Nations used military force to intervene in a dispute.

Rosa Parks Sits Firm

On December 1, 1955, Rosa Parks accidentally made history on her way home from work. Parks was an African-American woman living in Montgomery, Alabama. The buses were **segregated**—there were different sections for white and black passengers. She was sitting in the middle section, where black passengers were allowed if no white person needed to sit down. All went well until the white section filled up and a white man demanded Parks's seat. Parks was tired after her long day's work, and she did not want to stand. She refused to move.

This simple yet courageous act set in motion a whole chain of events as African Americans rallied to her support. They boycotted the buses by refusing to ride in them for 382 days. This caused the bus company to lose money.

Dr. Martin Luther King, Jr. helped organize the boycott. Before long, he was leading a civil rights movement to end segregation and get African Americans the same treatment as whites. The movement gained strength each year and resulted in the Civil Rights Act of 1964.

World Events

Pearson Awarded Nobel Prize

Lester B. Pearson was awarded the 1957 Nobel Peace Prize for his role in ending the Suez Crisis. He was the first Canadian to win the peace prize.

Pearson Helps End the Suez Crisis

The Suez Crisis began in July 1956. President Nasser of Egypt seized the Suez Canal from the British and French company that ran it. In response, Britain, France, and Israel attacked Egypt. As the conflict continued, people feared it would draw in other countries. A solution was suggested by Lester B. Pearson, Canada's secretary of state for external affairs. He proposed that a peacekeeping force be sent into the area to keep the warring sides apart. This force would be a United Nations army, composed of soldiers from several countries. The United Nations agreed to Pearson's plan, and the fighting stopped on November 6, 1956. A Canadian officer, General E.L.M. Burns, was the first commander of the peacekeeping army, which became known as the United Nations Emergency Force.

▌About 6,000 soldiers from 11 countries made up the United Nations Emergency Force.

Ghana Is Born

On March 6, 1957, the British **colony** in Africa known as the Gold Coast became an independent nation called Ghana. The event was celebrated throughout the country. Piling into buses, trains, and trucks, families rushed to the capital, Accra. Other families celebrated in their towns and villages. At the ceremonies in Accra, Prime Minister Kwame Nkrumah welcomed guests from 72 countries, including Canada. Ghana was the first black African colony to gain independence.

"By our actions, the whole future of Africa will be affected. We must not disappoint those millions of people to whom our success or failure will mean so much."
—Kwame Nkrumah

Castro Takes Over in Cuba

Amid cheering crowds, Fidel Castro rode triumphantly into Havana, Cuba, on January 8, 1959. His arrival marked the end of his two-year rebellion against the corrupt government of President Fulgencio Batista. Batista had fled, and Castro was now in charge. Most Cubans were feeling hopeful about the future.

Castro promised to make life better for the poor, and most Cubans were desperately poor. About 600,000 people did not have a job. Many had never been to school. Most Cubans did not even know how to read and write. Castro said he would provide free education for all children. He said he would build hospitals and other facilities, and he would take land from the rich and give it to **peasants**.

For years, Americans and other foreigners had run many of Cuban businesses, paying Cuban workers small wages. This would no longer be allowed, said Castro. In future, Cuba would be run by Cubans for the benefit of Cubans.

Fidel Castro led the Cuban government from 1959 to 2008.

The Hungarian Revolution Fails

Hungary had been a **republic** since 1946. Then, Hungarian communists began taking over the government. Most Hungarians did not want their country to be communist, and in 1956 they rebelled. People demanded democracy for their country. Their brave attempt was doomed when leading communists asked the Soviet Union for help. Soviet tanks rolled into Hungary and quickly put an end to the uprising.

European Economic Community

In 1958, the Treaty of Rome established the European Economic Community (EEC). Six nations belonged to this community: Belgium, France, Germany, Italy, Luxembourg, and the Netherlands. These countries had a "common market," which allowed goods to pass from one country to another without payment of customs duties. This made trade between the countries easier.

It was a big step for countries that had often been at war with each other. The six had begun to work together in 1952, when they made an agreement about their coal and steel industries. They recognized that Europeans had common goals and could benefit from cooperation. The EEC was the forerunner of today's European Union, which includes many more European countries.

The Hungarian rebellion lasted 13 days before Soviet forces brought the conflict to an end.

Canadian Decades 1950s

Political Issues

The Roncarelli versus Duplessis case established that government officials are not above the law.

Duplessis Made to Pay Up

During his 18 years as premier of Quebec, Maurice Duplessis governed with a firm hand. Those who opposed him called him a **dictator**. They were thrilled when a restaurant owner won a lawsuit against the powerful leader.

The restaurant owner was Frank Roncarelli, a member of the religious group called Jehovah's Witnesses. Duplessis disliked this group because their religion was so different from his own. When Jehovah's Witnesses handed out pamphlets explaining their beliefs, Duplessis had them arrested. Roncarelli often paid the arrested people's bail so that they did not have to stay in prison while awaiting trial.

Duplessis did not like Roncarelli's interference, so he tried to put Roncarelli out of business by cancelling his restaurant's liquor licence. Roncarelli responded by suing the premier. He said the premier's cancellation of his liquor licence was an abuse of power. The judge agreed. In May 1951, the Quebec Superior Court ordered Duplessis to pay Roncarelli more than $33,000 in damages. This decision was called a triumph by all those who had been demanding greater freedom in Quebec.

20   Political Issues

Uproar Over Pipeline

The Liberal government of Prime Minister Louis St. Laurent was in trouble in May 1956. It was because of a pipeline that was needed to bring natural gas from Alberta to central Canada.

The pipeline was to be built by a private company that a senior government minister had helped set up. The trouble started when the minister asked Parliament to approve the project and to grant the pipeline company a loan of $80 million.

This caused an uproar because the company was run largely by American businessmen. People said that the Canadian government should not give loans to American businesses. American businesses should not be allowed to own such an important Canadian pipeline, they argued.

The natural gas pipeline from Alberta to central Canada was completed in October 1958.

When the matter was hotly debated in Parliament. However, the debate did not last long. The government set a time limit on the debate. This made Canadians even angrier. They believed the time limit made the debate **undemocratic**. Other parties in Parliament screamed their disapproval.

When the debate ended in June and the pipeline bill was passed, the government seemed to have won. However, many Canadians now believed that the Liberals had been in power too long. They had forgotten to listen to Canadians. This paved the way for a Conservative government in 1957.

The Man From Prince Albert

In the federal election of 1957, the Liberals had a nasty surprise. After 22 years in power, they were turned out of office. The new prime minister was Conservative leader John G. Diefenbaker, "the man from Prince Albert." Diefenbaker had made his name as a lawyer in Prince Albert, Saskatchewan, before he entered Parliament.

Diefenbaker had great support among working people. One of his aims was to see that all Canadians were treated equally. "One Canada!" was Diefenbaker's rallying cry. Yet he knew he would have difficulty carrying out his policies. Diefenbaker's party had only a few more seats in Parliament than the Liberals. If the other parties sided with the Liberals, they would be able to outvote the Conservatives. In 1958, Diefenbaker decided to hold an early election to try to increase the number of Conservative seats.

> "Sir John A. Macdonald opened the West. He saw Canada from east to west. I see a new Canada—a Canada of the North!"
> —John Diefenbaker

John G. Diefenbaker led the Conservative Party to its first federal election victory in 27 years.

Canadian Decades 1950s

Political Issues

Conservative Landslide

The 1958 federal election was a landslide victory for the Conservative Party. Never before had any party won so many seats in Parliament. The Conservatives won 208 seats in the March 31 election. Prime Minister Diefenbaker now had a clear mandate to carry out his ideas for Canada. One plan was his "vision of the North." Diefenbaker planned to open up the Canadian North by building roads and railways, and by setting up research projects in the Arctic. Another key project was a bill of rights that would protect the disadvantaged or anyone who was different. In 1960, the Canadian Bill of Rights became law. It guaranteed all Canadians basic rights, such as freedom of speech and freedom to practise one's own religion.

Liberal Losses in the Maritimes

Most Nova Scotians could hardly remember a time when the Liberals did not govern their province. There had been Liberal governments since 1933. Much the same was true of Prince Edward Island, where the Liberals had been in power since 1935. The 1950s saw a change in both provinces. The Conservatives were voted into power in Nova Scotia in 1956 and in Prince Edward Island in 1959. The new premier of Nova Scotia was Robert Stanfield, who later became leader of the Progressive Conservative Party of Canada.

Senator James Gladstone

In 1958, Diefenbaker appointed James Gladstone to the Senate. Gladstone was the first **Aboriginal** person to become a senator. He had been president of the Indian Association of Alberta for many years and had often negotiated with the government. During his first speech in Parliament, Senator Gladstone spoke in the Blackfoot language. He did this, "in recognition of the First Canadians."

As president of the Indian Association of Alberta, James Gladstone had travelled to Ottawa three times to fight for Aboriginal rights.

Robert Stanfield led the Progressive Conservative Party from 1967 to 1976. He resigned after failing to lead the party to an election victory.

22 Political Issues

Women in Politics

The 1950s saw women playing a larger role in politics. In 1951, Thérèse Casgrain was elected leader of Quebec's social democratic party, the CCF. This made her the first woman ever to lead a political party in Canada. Then there was Ellen Fairclough from Hamilton, Ontario, whom Diefenbaker appointed to the cabinet in 1957. She was the first female Cabinet minister in the federal government. Another first was Charlotte Whitton, Ottawa's first female mayor. Nobody could overlook Mayor Whitton. Even the Lord Mayor of London was cut down to size when he tried to be coy with her, asking: "If I smell your corsage, will you blush?" Whitton shot back immediately: "If I pull your chain, will you flush?"

▎Charlotte Whitton was the first woman elected as mayor of a major Canadian city. She served as mayor of Ottawa from 1951 to 1956 and again from 1960 to 1964.

War Hero Made Governor General

In 1959, Major-General Georges Vanier was appointed governor general of Canada. He was the second Canadian-born governor general and the first French Canadian ever to hold the position. Vanier was greatly respected, and not only for his bravery in World War I. He had served Canada in many ways and was ambassador to France from 1944 to 1953.

"Striving, striving, and more striving" was the secret of success, in Major-General Vanier's view. He added, "I almost prefer striving without success to success without striving."

Canadian Decades 1950s 23

Literature

Farley Mowat

"Writing books for young people has been fun," said Farley Mowat. "It has brought me—and, I hope my young readers—the feeling that life is very much worth living." Mowat's first book for young people was *Lost in the Barrens*, which won the 1956 Governor General's Award. It is an adventure story about two boys who became friends. One is **Aboriginal**. The other is not. When they get lost in the Barren Lands of the Arctic, they survive because of their different skills, which they share with one another.

The following year, Mowat wrote one of his most popular books, *The Dog Who Wouldn't Be*. It is a story about Mutt, who had been Mowat's family pet when he was a boy in Saskatchewan. Mutt was always causing trouble. He chased cows. He chewed gum and swallowed it. He hated being washed, so he ate the soap.

Mutt reappears in *Owls in the Family*, another popular story. Two other Mowat books for young people are *The Curse of the Viking Grave* and *The Black Joke*. Some of the books Mowat wrote for adults have also been enjoyed by young readers. They include *A Whale for the Killing* and *Virunga*, the story of Dian Fossey and the mountain gorillas of Central Africa.

Farley Mowat's books have been translated into 52 languages.

Anne Hébert

Quebec poet Anne Hébert wrote her first collection of poems in 1942. She then wrote scripts for the National Film Board and broadcasts for Radio-Canada in 1954. She released her first novel in 1958. By the time it was translated into English as *The Silent Rooms*, she had written her best-known novel, *Kamouraska*. This story, which is based on a murder in 19th-century Quebec, was made into a popular film. It also earned her France's Prix des Libraires award. While continuing to write novels, Hébert also enhanced her reputation as a poet, winning many prizes in both Canada and France. Younger poets have been greatly influenced by her style of writing.

Morley Callaghan

When Morley Callaghan first began writing stories, he showed some of them to his American friend, Ernest Hemingway. Like Hemingway, he aimed to become a successful writer. He was encouraged when Hemingway told him, "You write big-time stuff. All you have to do is keep on writing."

Callaghan did keep on writing, and he eventually became famous. One reviewer called him "the most important novelist and short story writer in English Canada."

Callaghan's *The Loved and the Lost* earned him the 1951 Governor General's Award for fiction.

Hugh MacLennan Does it Again

The Watch that Ends the Night won Hugh MacLennan his fifth Governor General's Award in 1959. A story about moral courage, it has been called "the great Canadian novel." Yet MacLennan's best-known novel is probably Two Solitudes, about English-French relations in Canada. The term "two solitudes" has become a common phrase used to describe the relationship between English-speaking Canada and Quebec.

Hugh MacLennan published seven novels from 1941 to 1980.

GOVERNOR GENERAL'S AWARD

In 1959, the "Juvenile" category was dropped from the Governor General's Literary Awards. Consequently, there were only nine winners in the 1950s:

1950	Donalda Dickie, *The Great Adventure*
1951	John F. Hayes, *A Land Divided*
1952	Marie McPhedran, *Cargoes on the Great Lakes*
1953	John F. Hayes, *Rebels Ride at Night*
1954	Marjorie Wilkins Campbell, *The Nor'westers*
1955	Kerry Wood, *The Map-maker*
1956	Farley Mowat, *Lost in the Barrens*
1957	Kerry Wood, *The Great Chief*
1958	Edith L. Sharp, *Nkwala*

Science and Technology

Dr. Wilfred Bigelow's method of lowering the temperature of operation patients led to advances in heart and brain surgery.

Groundhog Study Sparks Breakthrough in Surgery

Why would a heart surgeon do research on groundhogs? "We hoped to find the cooling agent that makes it possible for groundhogs to **hibernate** in winter," explained Dr. Wilfred Bigelow. He and his team at Toronto General Hospital spent eight years trying to discover how groundhogs lower their body temperature for hibernation. They never found the answer, but they did find a way of making a patient's body very cold before an operation. This process, called **hypothermia**, opened up new opportunities in surgery. When a body is very cold, it uses far less oxygen. This means that longer and more complex operations can be done with greater safety. Surgeons throughout the world were quick to copy the Toronto method, which was first used in an open-heart operation in 1952. "We've started a new Ice Age," says Dr. Bigelow.

New Hope for Cancer Patients

The cobalt-60 machine was a new way of treating cancer with **radiation**. Invented by Dr. Harold Johns and his team at the University of Saskatchewan, it was first used on patients in the early 1950s. The cobalt-60 "bomb," as it was called, enabled doctors to treat cancers that were deep inside a patient's body. Previously, radiation treatment could be given only to cancers near the surface. The invention gave new hope to cancer patients.

▌The cobalt-60 resulted in cancer treatment success rates rising by as much as 50 percent.

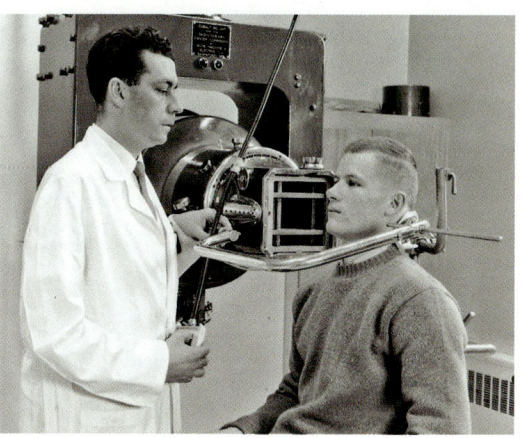

St. Lawrence Seaway opened

A triumph of engineering was celebrated on June 26, 1959, when the St. Lawrence Seaway was officially opened. Taking part in the event were Queen Elizabeth II, Prime Minister John Diefenbaker, and American President Dwight D. Eisenhower. As part of the opening ceremonies, they sailed through St. Lambert Lock, at Montreal, in the royal yacht *Britannia*. Hundreds of balloons, rockets, fireworks, and flags were released for the 15,000 people who had come to celebrate.

SEAWAY FACTS
- the finished canal was 3,770 kilometres long
- work began in 1954 using both Canadian and American crews
- between Montreal and Lake Ontario, seven locks raise ships 68 metres
- by the end of the seaway, a ship is raised 183 metres above sea level

Sports

Canada's Best All-Round Athletes

Lionel Conacher, the "Big Train," was chosen Canada's all-round athlete of the half century in 1950. Canada's all-round female athlete of the half century was Bobbie (Fanny) Rosenfeld.

The Big Train was an obvious choice. He had made his name in wrestling, boxing, football, lacrosse, baseball, and hockey. Sometimes, he played in two different games on the same day, dashing from one to the other. One story says that he helped the Toronto Hillcrest team win the Ontario baseball championship by hitting a triple in the final inning. He then drove across town to help his lacrosse team with a championship. He scored four of his team's goals in that game. Conacher later played professional football and hockey.

Bobbie Rosenfeld also shone in numerous sports, including softball, basketball, hockey, track and field, and tennis. She won the 1924 Toronto grass-courts tennis title and set new records for the long jump. Her peak performance was in the 1928 Olympic Games, when she won a silver medal in the 100-metre dash and a gold medal in the 400-metre relay. One admirer recalled, "She was not big, perhaps five-foot-five. She didn't look powerful, but she was wiry and quick. Above all, she was aggressive, very aggressive physically....She simply went after everything with full force." In later life, she wrote a sports column called Sports Reel for the *Globe and Mail*.

> "He was probably the greatest athlete I have ever coached in football or any other form of athletics."
> —Conacher's coach

■ Today, the Canadian Press presents the Lionel Conacher Award and the Bobbie Rosenfeld Award to the best male and female athletes in the country each year.

Marilyn Bell Swims Lake Ontario

"I'll never say a woman can't do anything in the future," said a Toronto taxi driver. Sixteen-year-old Marilyn Bell had just done what no one else had ever managed. She had swum across Lake Ontario, a distance of 52 kilometres. Americans and Canadians had been trying to cross the lake for years. Nobody dreamed that a Canadian high school student would be the first to succeed. Entering the water at midnight on September 8, 1954, Marilyn swam through the rest of the night and all the next day. She struggled ashore near the Canadian National Exhibition grounds on the evening of September 9. Marilyn was so exhausted that she was hardly aware of the cheering crowds who had gathered to greet her. The radio had been broadcasting news of her progress, and 250,000 people had flocked to the waterfront to celebrate her arrival. The swim took Bell 20 hours and 59 minutes to complete.

■ In 1955, Marilyn Bell became the youngest person ever to swim across the English Channel. A year later, she swam across the Straight of Juan de Fuca.

Riot Ends Hockey Game

On March 17, 1955, angry hockey fans went wild at the Montreal Forum, hurling eggs, tomatoes, and peanuts at Clarence Campbell, the National Hockey League president. Campbell had suspended Maurice "The Rocket" Richard for attacking a player and a linesman the previous Sunday. The fans were outraged at this treatment of their idol. They became so violent that the game had to be stopped. As people poured out of the Forum, they were joined by thousands of other angry Montrealers. The mob spread along St. Catherine Street, smashing shop windows and anything else in their path. By midnight, more than 100 people had been arrested.

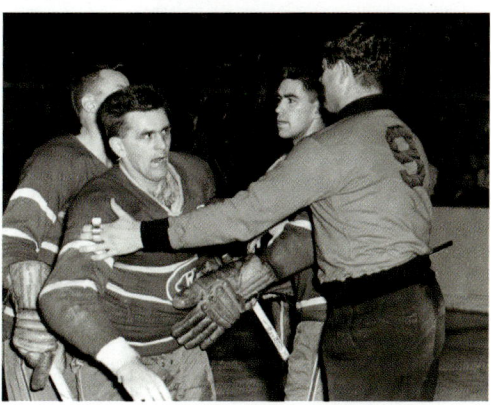

■ Many people in Montreal felt Maurice Richard's suspension was too severe.

Grey Cup Game Shown on TV

On November 29, 1952, the Grey Cup game was shown on television for the first time. More than 700,000 fans were able to watch the Toronto Argonauts play the Edmonton Eskimos at Varsity Stadium in Toronto. The picture was clear, but it failed during the third quarter. Fortunately, the sound was not affected. The announcer continued to describe the game while a technician climbed a 100-metre tower to repair a receiver. The picture came back 29 minutes later, in time for viewers to see the exciting finish. The score was 21–11 in favour of the Argonauts.

Sports

Rowing Team Wins Gold Medal

A four-oar crew from British Columbia won a gold medal at the Olympic Games in Australia in 1956. This was the first time Canada had ever won an Olympic rowing event. The four members of the crew were Don Arnold, Lorne Loomer, Walter d'Hondt, and Archie McKinnon. Until a few months before the event, only 21-year-old Don Arnold had any rowing experience. The other three were 19 and had never rowed before. They were trained by former rower Frank Read. "He is fantastic the way he can inspire us," said Walter d'Hondt of his coach. "He makes us want to do anything for him." The crew members rowed from 5:00 to 6:30 a.m., worked all day as construction workers, and then rowed another hour and a half in the evenings. On weekends, they rowed long distances under the watchful eye of Read.

Read commented that the team's success "was the most phenomenal effort ever made in international competition."

■ Canada's rowers set an Olympic record in 1956 when they defeated the United States by five lengths.

Canadian Pairs Are the Tops

Canadian pairs figure skaters were the best in the world in the late 1950s and early 1960s. Both Barbara Wagner and Robert Paul were late starters in figure skating. Wagner began at 13 years of age and Paul at 10 as part of his recovery from childhood **polio**.

Wagner and Paul dominated the scene, remaining world champions from 1957 to 1960, and winning the gold medal at the 1960 Olympic Games. Not far behind Wagner and Paul were the brother and sister pair, Maria and Otto Jelinek. The Jelineks had immigrated to Canada from Czechoslovakia with their family after World War II. The Jelineks won the Canadian junior pairs title in 1955, and in 1962 they won the world championship. Both pairs had the reputation of being dedicated professionals.

■ After their 1960 Olympic gold medal, Barbara Wagner and Robert Paul continued to skate professionally until 1964.

30 Sports

A First for Goalies

With blood pouring from his face, goalie Jacques Plante was helped off the ice. The puck had hit him square on the nose. "We've had it now," muttered a Montreal Canadiens fan. There seemed to be nothing left to stop the New York Rangers from sweeping to victory. The Canadiens did not have a spare goalie for the game on November 2, 1959.

As Plante sat in the dressing room while the cut on his nose was sewn up, coach Toe Blake tried to persuade him to go back on the ice. Plante refused. He said he would only go back if he could wear the mask he had been using in practices. At that time, goaltenders did not wear masks in games, and Blake was against it. Nevertheless, Plante won the argument, and the Canadiens won the game. From then on, Plante always wore a protective mask when he was in goal. Soon, other goalies began to do so, too.

▌Jacques Plante was the first goaltender in the NHL to wear a mask on a regular basis.

Marlene Stewart

"No other Canadian golfer, man or woman, has ever run up a series of victories comparable to hers," wrote sports columnist Jack Batten.

Marlene Stewart started working as a caddy when she was 12 years old. She loved the sport as soon as she tried it. The club's pro once commented that he could not go into the pro shop without tripping over Stewart's shoes. She got her first hole in one when she was 15. The rest is gold history.

Between 1951 and 1973, Stewart won the Canadian Ladies' Open Amateur championship 11 times. In 1956, she won 34 matches in a row. These wins included the Canadian Open and the United States Women's Amateur championship. A journalist once said, "She is a perfectionist...she has hit more golf shots, mostly in practice, in her three years in the game than the vast majority of women golfers have hit in the last 10."

▌Marlene Stewart is a member of the World Golf Hall of Fame.

Economy

Canada's forestry industry boomed in the 1950s, especially in British Columbia.

Economy Booming

The 1950s were great times for Canada. There were plenty of jobs, and people had money to spend. In Ontario and Quebec especially, new factories and businesses employed thousands of people. Many others found work in the forestry and mining industries.

Even parts of the country that had been hit hard by the Depression of the 1930s were doing well. In Atlantic Canada, for instance, numerous businesses were started. As well, the new, large military base at Gagetown, New Brunswick, provided many jobs. However, the picture was not so bright in Newfoundland, where most people still had a hard time making a living.

By contrast, Western Canada was booming. Alberta was doing especially well because of the huge deposits of oil and gas that had been discovered there. Copper, zinc, and uranium mines were adding to Saskatchewan's **revenue**, while new hydroelectric plants and other developments were bringing jobs to British Columbia and Manitoba. The outlook was also good for prairie farmers because the federal government was selling large quantities of wheat abroad.

Avro Arrow Cancelled

"It can't be true!" said an aircraft mechanic, but it was true. In February 1959, Prime Minister Diefenbaker cancelled all work on Canada's famous jet fighter plane, the Avro Arrow. He said it was costing too much money. The military no longer seemed interested in fighter planes—missiles seemed to be a better defence. The whole project was scrapped. The few planes already built were to be destroyed, said Diefenbaker.

This was a major blow to Canada's aircraft industry. The Arrow was a magnificent plane. Test flights had indicated it would be one of the fastest fighter planes in the world—test planes had gone almost twice the speed of sound. There had been talk of building 600 Arrows, and now not even one would exist. About 14,000 people lost their jobs.

At a cost of $12.5 million per plane, the Canadian government decided the Avro Arrow was too expensive and scrapped the project.

Equal Pay for Some Women

As a rule, men earned far more money than women. In 1950, for example, the average salary of a Canadian man was $2,419. For a Canadian woman, it was $1,376. Many people thought this was fair and proper. "Men have to support a family," they said. "Men ought to get paid more." Women's groups disagreed, and they pressed for change. They had some success in 1951, when the Ontario government passed a law stating that women must be paid the same as men if they did the same job. Five years later, the federal government passed a similar law, but it applied only to people working for the federal government.

Labour Relations

In 1956, Canada's two main union organizations joined together to form the Canadian Labour Congress (CLC). The CLC represented most Canadian workers who belonged to a union.

Huge Uranium Find at Elliot Lake

In 1954, the discovery of uranium at Elliot Lake, Ontario, sparked a mining boom. People flocked to the area. At a height of the boom, mine-shaft drillers could earn as much as $1,200 a month—about six times more than the average Canadian salary. Before long, there were 11 mines in operation, including Consolidated Denison, the world's largest uranium mine.

Canadian Decades 1950s

Fashion

Stiletto Heels

In the late 1950s, the stiletto-heeled shoe, with its pointed "winkle-picker" toe, was very popular. Not everyone enjoyed this new fashion trend, however. The spiky heels ruined carpets and made little dents in wooden floors. They were even worse on linoleum. Some doctors joined the campaign against them, pointing out that winkle-pickers crushed women's toes. Saddle shoes and penny loafers were far better for the feet, they said. Loafers and saddle shoes were popular, although most young women wanted to have at least one pair of stilettos.

■ Stiletto-heeled shoes were made in many colours and materials so that they would match a woman's hat, gloves, and handbag.

Poodle skirts

Most young women had a closet full of poodle skirts. These skirts were ironed regularly to keep them crisp. A crinoline, a stiff dress lining, was used to make the skirt flare out. This '50s clothing got its name from the image of a poodle sewn on the bottom of the skirt. Girls often wore these skirts with bobby socks and running shoes. But some women preferred a different style. Tight-fitting skirts were also popular in the 1950s. A fitted jacket was often worn to complete the look.

■ Poodle skirts were most common among teenagers, who often wore them to school dances.

When to Wear a Hat

Although no longer a "must" for everyday wear, a hat was still considered an essential part of a woman's outfit for many occasions. A well-dressed woman wore matching gloves, shoes, and handbag, even to go shopping. In the summer, these accessories would all be white. Most women still wore a hat in church or the synagogue. However, hats were worn less often than in the 1940s. Women could go hatless at informal lunch parties. Young women, especially, often went without a hat.

■ Women's hat fashion in the 1950s included a wide range of styles, from wide brims to no brims at all, and everything in between.

Fifties Fashions

American film stars and other celebrities set the style for many Canadians. On formal occasions, young women wore strapless dresses with swirling skirts, like Marilyn Monroe. Straight skirts were also popular. Whether skirts were full or straight, they came halfway down the calf. Young men also copied the stars in the way they dressed. Some of them slicked back their hair and tried to look like Elvis Presley or James Dean. **Crew cuts** were popular with others. Men's pants were baggy and often had cuffs. **Drip-dry** shirts were the latest thing, worn by both men and women.

James Dean and Marilyn Monroe set the fashion pace for North American men and women.

Canadian Decades 1950s 35

Immigration

▎Many Asian immigrants in the 1950s settled in Vancouver, British Columbia

Asian Immigration

By the 1950s, most of Canada's restrictions against Chinese immigration had been removed. About 2,000 Chinese people immigrated each year. The situation was very different for people from the Indian subcontinent. The Immigration Act of 1951 set a tiny **quota**: 150 from India each year, 100 from Pakistan, and 50 from Sri Lanka. These numbers were gradually increased over the years but not by much.

Many Canadians approved of these restrictions. They wanted Canada to be mainly British, or at least European. However, a few Canadians who had lived in India had other ideas. One Canadian said, "The present policy is very unfair. After all, we are fellow members of the British Commonwealth." "The people are hard workers and make good citizens," said another. He added that Canadian food could be less dull if Canada had more immigrants from Asia. "Have you ever seen a mango for sale in the supermarket?" he asked. "Of course not! And if you want a good curry, forget it. Even big cities like Toronto and Montreal don't have an Indian restaurant."

British Immigrants Are Pouring In

"By golly, there's no snow!" said an Englishman as he stepped off the boat in Montreal. Perhaps he was joking. The ship bringing him from England had enjoyed warm July weather as it sailed up the St. Lawrence River. But the Englishman was heading for Elliot Lake, Ontario, which does have very cold winters. He had been warned about the winters when applying for a job in Elliot Lake's uranium mines.

This man was one of the many British immigrants who poured into Canada. More immigrants arrived from the British Isles than from anywhere else. The government favoured French and British immigrants because they spoke the same language as Canadians and had many of the same traditions. But far more Britons than French come to Canada. In 1957, for example, more than 100,000 immigrants were from Britain while less than 6,000 were from France. Unlike the French, the British saw Canada as a "home away from home." It was much the same, only better, because jobs were easier to find. "Canada is a land of opportunity," said one new arrival.

■ The Canadian Embassy in London, England, was swarmed with hundreds of people hoping to emigrate to Canada in the 1950s.

Total Immigrants

The Suez Crisis of 1956, the failed Hungarian revolution, and the possibility of war in Europe caused a large number of Europeans to move to Canada in the late 1950s. These events explain the steep rise in immigration numbers in 1957.

IMMIGRANTS TO CANADA

Year	Immigrants
1950	73,912
1951	194,391
1952	164,498
1953	168,868
1954	154,227
1955	109,946
1956	164,857
1957	282,164
1958	124,851
1959	106,928

Hungarians Arrive in Canada

More than 37,000 Hungarians found a new home in Canada in the late 1950s. As Soviet tanks rolled into Hungary to crush the uprising against communism, thousands of people fled across the border into Austria. Many of them were university students. Others were writers, artists, or teachers. Most were highly educated and soon found work in Canada.

Canadian Decades 1950s

Music and the Arts

At the age of 10, Glen Gould began studying music at the Royal Conservatory. By 14, he was playing with the Toronto Symphony Orchestra.

A Brilliant Young Pianist

Glenn Gould's 1955 recording of Johann Sebastian Bach's Goldberg Variations brought him worldwide attention. He was called one of the greatest pianists of the day. Gould was only 23 years old, yet he was already well known to Canadian music lovers. Many had heard him on the radio or attended his concerts. He had first performed on CBC radio in 1952.

The critics raved about Gould's playing. It was clear and precise. His technique was superb, they said, and he played with wonderful delicacy. Yet many could not understand Gould's strange personal style at performances. He always brought his own chair to concerts, and he sat very low, so that he seemed to be crouching over the piano. Also, he hummed while he played. This was unusual, but his talent made his odd habits more acceptable.

A Superb Choir

When conductor Elmer Iseler helped found the Toronto Festival Singers in 1954, he started something great. This was choral singing at its best. If people could not get to Toronto to hear the choir, they could catch it on CBC radio or television.

▎Elmer Iseler often toured with his choirs to promote Canadian music.

▎Elvis Presley was almost as well known for his dancing as he was for his singing.

"Our Pet, Juliette"

It was partly because she looked so young and innocent that she was known as "Our Pet, Juliette." Born of Ukrainian-Polish parents, Juliette Sysak was only 15 years old when she first sang on CBC radio. She quickly gained a large number of fans, and she was soon appearing regularly on country music shows.

Before long, Sysak had her own show, *Here's Juliette*. Like many other radio stars, Sysak moved over to television in the early 1950s. During the late 1950s, her show *Juliette* was one of the most popular programs on CBC television. "She's so warm and folksy," said an admirer. "That's Juliette's charm. You feel she's one of the family."

Is the Face Familiar?

If you took a taxi in Montreal in the 1950s, you might have recognized the driver. It could have been Jean Carignan, the well-known fiddle player. "Ti-Jean" gave up playing with Bob Hill's dance band in 1956 and chose to earn his living by driving a cab. This seemed to benefit his playing. At folk festivals and concerts, he tossed off jigs and reels and traditional songs with tremendous energy. He was forced to retire in 1978 because he lost his hearing.

Elvis Is Here

The noise was deafening. "Elvis, I love you!" screamed a young girl in bobby socks. Elvis Presley was visiting Canada for the first time on April 3, 1957, and it seemed that half the country had come to welcome the American rock star. Thousands of teenagers crowded into Toronto's Maple Leaf Gardens. They screamed with delight as "Elvis the Pelvis" twirled his hips and flung himself around the stage. The screams almost drowned out Elvis's singing.

Paul Anka a Big Hit

Elvis Presley was not the only hit in town. Canada's Paul Anka became a teen idol around the same time. His 1957 recording Diana rocketed him to fame at just 15 years of age. When Anka set off on a tour of Britain that December, he was mobbed by teenage girls wherever he went. He was given the same noisy reception on his 1958 tour of Australia and Japan.

During the following years, Anka gained fame as a songwriter even more than a singer. My Way, which he wrote for Frank Sinatra, was one of his most famous songs. Another major hit was She's a Lady.

▎Paul Anka wrote more than 400 songs, many of which became hits.

Canadian Decades 1950s

Society

Beatniks set themselves apart from the mainstream culture of the 1950s by rejecting the popular fashion, music, and art of the day.

Dig It

"They are just dirty people wearing sandals," said their critics. **Beatniks** were a lot more than that, however. To be sure, many of them did wear sandals. The men generally had beards. The women favoured peasant skirts and black woolen stockings. If you went into any of the new coffee bars in the 1950s, you could spot them easily. They were certainly not dressed for the office. But that was the point. Beatniks were against the organized, traditional way most people lived. Beatniks were not interested in making money. Poetry and art were "where it was at." Coffee shops and late-night clubs often gave "beat" poets the stage to recite their work. When not writing or reading poetry, beatniks took pride in "bugging the squares."

Baby Boom

They called it the Baby Boom. During the late 1950s and early 1960s, a record number of babies were born in Canada. During World War II, few couples had children. Now times were different. Couples were together again, there were plenty of jobs available, and the future seemed bright. Young people wanted to settle down, get married, and raise a family. That is exactly what many did.

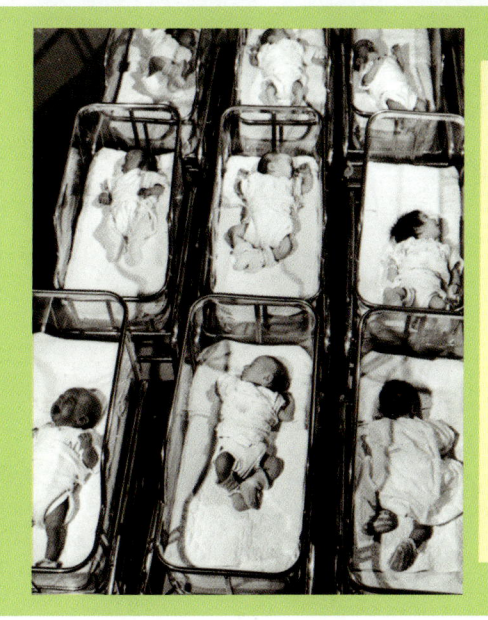

TOTAL NUMBER OF BIRTHS	
1950	372,009
1951	381,092
1952	403,559
1953	417,884
1954	436,198
1955	442,937
1956	450,739
1957	469,093
1958	470,118
1959	479,275

A Vaccine Against Polio

In 1954, people throughout North America breathed a great sigh of relief. The polio **epidemic** was over thanks to a new **vaccine**.

Poliomyelitis, also known as infantile paralysis, killed or crippled thousands each year. In 1953, about 8,000 Canadians caught polio, and 481 died of the disease. Many of those who survived could not walk without a brace. In 1954, a vaccine developed by the American researcher Dr. Jonas Salk became widely available. As a result, only 157 Canadians died from polio that year. The numbers dropped as more people were injected with the Salk vaccine.

Inuit Moved to High Arctic

"The government is anxious to have Canadians occupying as much of the north as possible," said a spokesperson for the federal government. He was explaining why groups of Inuit were being moved to the High Arctic. The government wanted to be sure the Canadian Arctic remained Canadian. Politicians and military people were worried about both American and Soviet Union interest in the region. Fifty-three Inuit were taken to that icy region in August 1953, and more were sent later.

The High Arctic is the part of Canada nearest the North Pole. It consists of bare, windswept islands. The government chose the Inuit as the people to go there because Inuit know how to survive in the Arctic. "They have skills that other Canadians lack," said the government spokesperson. He seemed unaware that most of the animals hunted by Inuit lived farther south. The Inuit who were sent to the High Arctic had a terrible time. They suffered from bitter cold, loneliness, and starvation. Some did not survive.

Traditions No Longer Banned

In 1951, a revision to Canada's Indian Act lifted the ban on the Sun Dance, **Potlatch**, and other traditional ceremonies. Since 1884, these ceremonies had been banned. People caught participating could be arrested.

▎The Sun Dance is an Aboriginal ceremony that often brings many Aboriginal groups together.

Canadian Decades 1950s 41

Canada/U.S. Relations

Niagara Agreement

In 1950, Canada and the United States signed an agreement about the water flowing over Niagara Falls. It was called the Niagara Diversion Treaty. Both nations used the Falls to produce electricity. For both nations, Niagara Falls was also an important tourist attraction. The treaty made sure that a certain amount of water would stay in the river and continue to flow over the falls. The remainder was to be divided equally between Canada and the United States. Canada's water was diverted from the Niagara River above the falls and channelled into electric-generating stations.

More than 565,000 litres of water pour over Niagara Falls every second.

DEW Line Completed

The Distant Early Warning (DEW) Line came into operation on July 31, 1957. The DEW Line is a network of radar stations in the North. It was the result of an agreement signed between Canada and the United States in 1955. The Americans were worried that Soviet bombers might launch a surprise attack by flying over the North Pole. In order to have plenty of warning of such an attack, they needed a chain of radar stations across the entire Arctic—the Canadian Arctic as well as Alaska. The DEW Line stations stretched from Alaska to Baffin Island.

Although the DEW Line protected Canada as well as the United States, some Canadians were not happy about the project. They pointed out that the radar stations were American military bases. Canadians could not enter them without permission. With the stations, they claimed, Americans had taken control of large tracts of the Canadian Arctic.

By the 1990s, the DEW Line had been replaced with the more advanced North Warning System, which could detect low-flying missiles.

Joint Defence Agreement

In 1958, Canada and the United States signed an agreement to create a joint force to protect North America. It was called the North American Air Defence Command (NORAD). The new defence force had its headquarters in Colorado Springs, Colorado, and was commanded by an American. His second-in-command was a senior officer in the Royal Canadian Air Force. It was agreed that NORAD would have about 200,000 soldiers, 17,000 of whom would be Canadians.

Advances in technology have made most of the original NORAD defense systems obsolete.

How Wide Is the Border?

In the 1950s, it sometimes seemed as though there was no border between the United States and Canada at all. Movies, television shows, books, music, fashions, ideas, hockey stars, and many other products moved north across the border easily.

The American movies *High Noon* and *On the Waterfront* were especially popular in Canada in the 1950s. Favourite film stars included James Dean, Grace Kelly, Marilyn Monroe, and Humphrey Bogart. Popular music ranged from cowboy songs to cool jazz. American musicals, such as Guys and Dolls, were also popular with Canadians. As for sports, Americans played on Canadian teams, and Canadians played on American teams. American tourists flocked into Canada, eager to enjoy such attractions as the Stratford Festival and the National Ballet.

American money also flowed across the border. This was partly because of the recent discovery of oil, uranium, and other resources in Canada. It was expensive to develop these resources, and Americans were eager to invest their money. Both countries benefited from the arrangement. But in the mid-1950s, a government report showed that Americans owned a large proportion of Canadian businesses. This worried many people. They said that Canada was turning into an American state.

Canadian Decades 1950s

Activities

Where did it happen?

Match the event to the place in Canada where it happened.

a) Coal-mining disaster
b) Opening of St. Lawrence Seaway
c) Red River flood
d) Big uranium discovery
e) Big military base established
f) Oil discoveries
g) Hometown of Prime Minister Diefenbaker

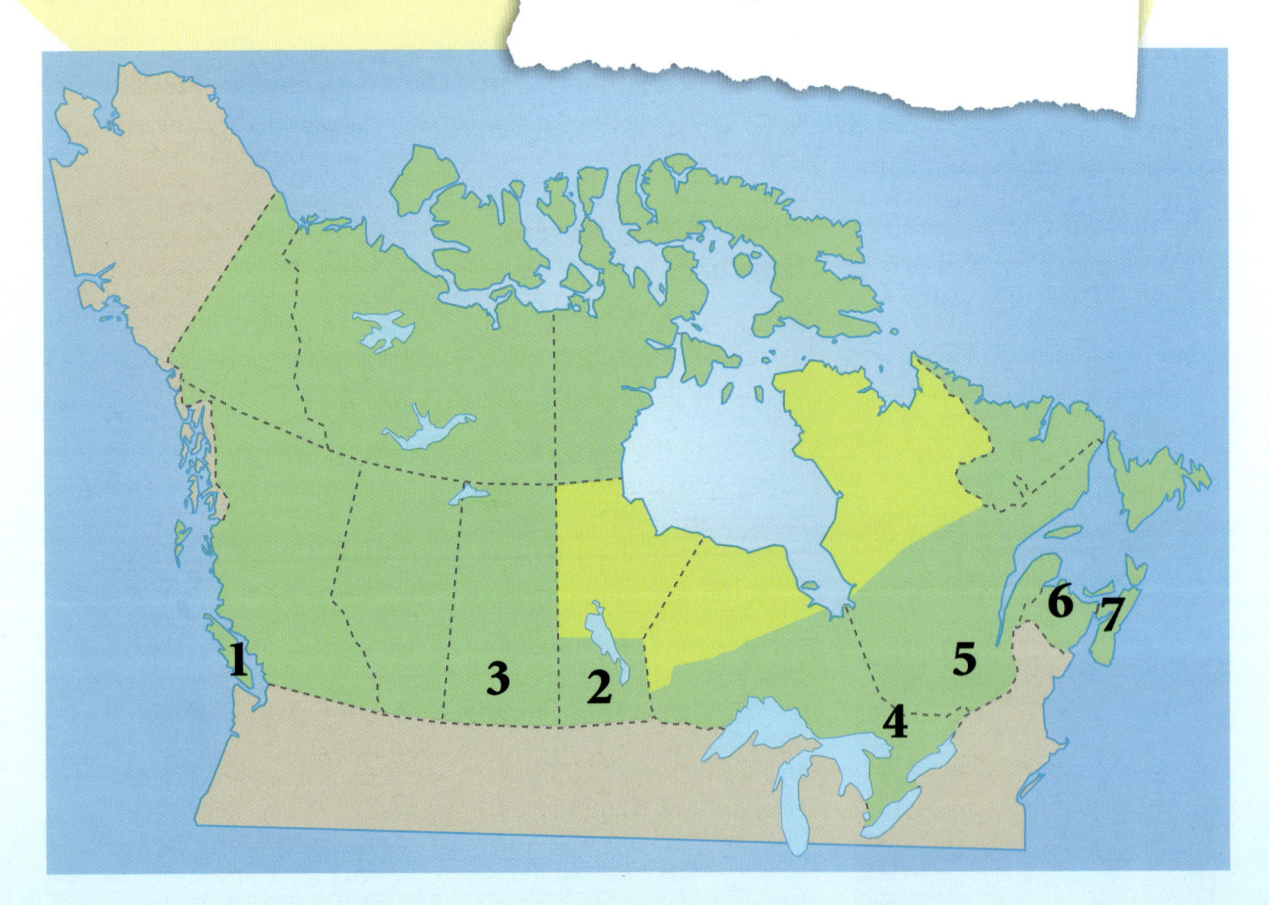

Answers: 1.c, 2.g, 3.f, 4.d, 5.b, 6.e, 7.a

44   Activities

Trivia Challenge

Match the following remarks to the people who said them:

1) "If I pull your chain, will you flush?"
   a) Joe Smith, to the governor general, when doing repairs at Rideau Hall
   b) Charlotte Whitton, mayor of Ottawa, when meeting a British visitor
   c) Comedian Frank Shuster, during a famous TV skit

2) "We have started a new Ice Age."
   a) A Toronto maker of Italian ice cream
   b) A sculptor at Quebec's Winter Carnival
   c) A Canadian heart surgeon

3) "I see a new Canada—a Canada of the North."
   a) Prime Minister John Diefenbaker
   b) One of the artists in the group Painters Eleven
   c) Joseph Hirshhorn of Elliot Lake uranium mines

Answers: 1. b; 2. c; 3. a

Newsmakers

Match the person with the province or territory:

a) Don Arnold, Lorne Loomer, Walter d'Hondt, and Archie McKinnon
b) Maurice Richard
c) John Hirsch
d) Elmer Iseler
e) John Diefenbaker
f) James Gladstone
g) Robert Stanfield

Saskatchewan
B.C.
Quebec
Alberta
Nova Scotia
British Columbia
Manitoba

Answers:
a. British Columbia
b. Quebec
c. Manitoba
d. Ontario
e. Saskatchewan
f. Alberta
g. Nova Scotia

Canadian Decades 1950s

Learning More

Here are some book resources and Internet links if you want to learn more about the people, places, and events that made headlines during the 1950s.

Books

Bond, Robert J., and William C. Mattys. *Years of Promise: Canada 1945–1963*. Canadian Scrapbook. Scarborough: Prentice-Hall of Canada, 1980.

Howard, Richard, Jacques Lacoursière, and Claude Bouchard. *A New History of Canada*. Vol. 12, World Presence: 1951–1960. Montreal: Editions Format, 1973.

Legrand, Jacques, and Elizabeth Abbott. *Chronicle of Canada*. Montreal: Chronicle Publications, 1990.

Ross, Alexander. *The Booming Fifties: 1950–1960. Canada's Illustrated Heritage.* Toronto: Natural Science of Canada, 1977.

The Junior Encyclopedia of Canada. Edmonton: Hurtig Publishers, 1990.

Internet Links

www.glenngould.com
Glenn Gould's official website provides more information on this a Canadian music legend.

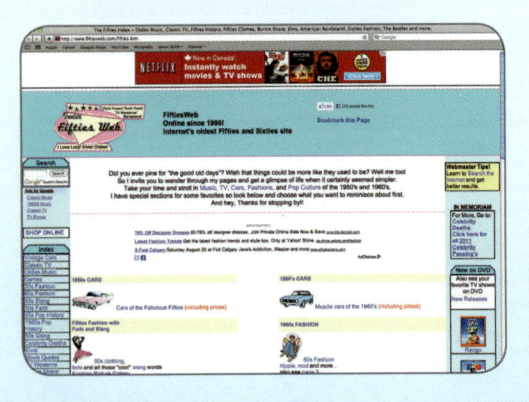

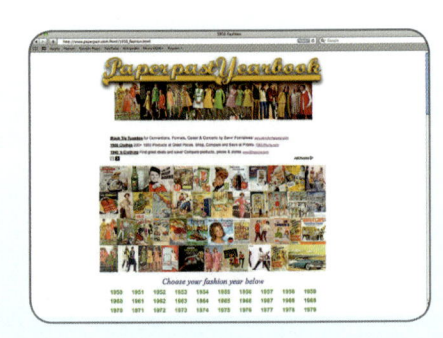

www.paperpast.com/html/1950_fashion.html
Learn more about 1950s fashion and trends at this site.

www.fiftiesweb.com/fifties.htm
Take a look at Fifties fads, fashion, cars, music and more on Fifties Web.

Learning More/Glossary

Glossary

Aboriginal: the original or earliest known inhabitants of a region or country

beatniks: people from the 1950s and early 1960s who acted against the accepted standards in dress, speech, and expression

cabinet: a group of government officials who serve as the heads of government departments

Canada Council: a government organization that encourages the study and enjoyment of the arts, humanities, and social sciences

celluloid: a strong plastic that is used as the base of motion picture film

colony: a territory that is far away from the country that governs it

communist: a system of leadership in which the government owns all property and goods and distributes them among its people

coronation: the ceremony of crowning a king or a queen

crew cut: a haircut for men or boys in which the hair is cut very short

demilitarized zone: an area where military activity is not permitted

dictator: a person who rules a country without sharing power

drip-dry: a type of clothing fabric that will dry with little wrinkling or creasing if it is hung up while wet

dykes: dams or high walls of earth that hold back water

epidemic: when a disease that affects many people at the same time in a region that does not usually suffer from that disease

expedition: a journey or voyage made for a specific reason

hibernate: when an animal lowers its body temperature during the winter to conserve energy

hypothermia: the condition of having a very low body temperature

peasants: a class of people often thought to be of low social rank, such as farmers or labourers

polio: an acute infectious disease caused by a virus

Potlatch: a major ceremony among many Aboriginal Peoples of the West Coast

quota: a set target to be reached

radiation: the process of using radioactive energy to treat disease

republic: form of government in which the authority belongs to the people

revenue: money made from property, investment, and taxes

revue: theatrical entertainment that includes singing and dancing

segregated: situation in which one racial group is set apart from another

slapstick: physical comedy that is rough and exaggerated

undemocratic: not in keeping with the principles of democracy

uranium: a radioactive substance, sometimes used for bombs

vaccine: a liquid containing the germs of a disease that helps the body protect itself from the same disease

Index

Anka, Paul 39
Arnold, Don 30, 45
Avro Arrow 33

baby boom 41
beatniks 40
Bell, Marilyn 29
Berton, Pierre 13
Bigelow, Wilfred 26
British Commonwealth 36
Bush, Jack 15

Cahén, Oscar 15
Callaghan, Morley 24
Canada Council 12, 13
Canadian Broadcasting Corporation (CBC) 12, 13, 38, 39
Canadian Labour Congress 33
cancer 27
Carignan, Jean 39
Casgrain, Thérèse 23
Castro, Fidel 19
civil rights 17
Cobalt 60 27
coffee shops 40
communism 17, 19, 37
Conacher, Lionel 28
Conservative Party 21, 22

Davis, Fred 13
DEW Line 43
d'Hondt, Walter 30, 45
Diefenbaker, John G. 21, 22, 23, 27, 33, 44, 45
Duplessis, Maurice 20

Elliot Lake 33, 37, 45
European Economic Community 19

Fairclough, Ellen 23
flood 9, 44
Franca, Celia 13

Gélinas, Gratien 11
Ghana 18
Gladstone, James 22, 45
Gordon, Hortense 15
Gould, Glenn 38, 46
Governor General's Award 24, 25
Grey Cup 29
Guthrie, Tyrone 11

Harron, Don 11
Hébert, Anne 25
Hendry, Tom 12
hibernation 26
Hirsch, John 12, 45
hula hoop 4, 15
Hungarian Revolution 19, 37
hurricane 9
hypothermia 26

Indian Act 40
Inuit 6, 41
Iseler, Elmer 39, 45

Jelinek, Maria and Otto 30
Johns, Harold 27

Korean War 17

Liberal Party 21, 22
Loomer, Lorne 30, 45

Macdonald, Jock 15
MacLennan, Hugh 25
Macpherson, Duncan 11
Manitoba Theatre Centre 12
McKinnon, Archie 30, 45
Mount Everest 17
Mowat, Farley 24, 25

Nakamura, Kazuo 15
Niagara Falls 42
Nobel Peace Prize 18
NORAD 43

Parks, Rosa 17
Patterson, Tom 11
Paul, Robert 30
Pearson, Lester 4, 18
pipeline 21
Plante, Jacques 31
polio 30, 41
Presley, Elvis 4, 35, 39

Quebec Winter Carnival 10
Queen Elizabeth II 16, 27

Read, Frank 30
Richard, Maurice 29, 45
riot 29
Ronald, William 15
Roncarelli, Frank 20
Rosenfeld, Bobbie 28

Shuster, Frank 12, 45
Spring Thaw 11
Springhill Mine disaster 8
St. Laurent, Louis 21

St. Lawrence Seaway 27, 44
Stanfield, Robert 22, 45
Stewart, Marlene 31
stiletto 34
Stratford Festival 11, 43
suburbs 4, 14
Suez Canal 18, 37
Sysak, Juliette 39

3-D movies 15
television 4, 9, 12, 13, 15, 29, 39, 43, 45
Tit-Coq 11
Town, Harold 15

vaccine 41
Vanier, Georges 23

Wagner, Barbara 30
Wayne, Johnny 12
Whitton, Charlotte 23, 45

48   Index